Inspirational Embroidery:

Stumpwork Flower Embroidery

Jill Kipnis

Over the years I have been teaching this craft, I have realised that technique is the foundation of the very best work. My aim is to share my knowledge and skills with you in this series, focusing on one technique at a time in order to help you build a platform to improve your own work.

I love stumpwork as it brings embroidery alive. When you use this book please think not only of the illustrated project but also the endless opportunities that this technique can be used for. You can easily create people, animals, insects and more!

Embroidery is a wonderful craft, and I've seen how it helps my students relax and unwind. I hope it helps you find your inner peace and a sense of satisfaction with what you have achieved.

If you would like any further information please visit my website: *www.inspirationalembroidery.co.uk*

Jill Kipnis

I grew up surrounded by fabrics and threads. My mother was always knitting, sewing and embroidering and I'm sure this had great influence on my passion for the craft of embroidery.

I have been lucky enough to serve an apprenticeship at *The Royal School of Needlework* This gave me a wonderful grounding in traditional hand techniques of embroidery. I also went on to gain a degree in Textiles & Fashion, which broadened my knowledge of design and free motion machine embroidery.

... look out for further books in this series to help you build confidence in not only technique but design.

Materials

Wire

There are many types of wires that can be used – from floral to picture wire. It depends on what colours and size your final piece will be but I like to use a fine black or silver wire for flowers and green wire for leaves.

A 30 gauge floral wire is good. Most craft dealers sell fine beading wires in a variety of colours. I used a 3mm silver beading wire in this project.

DMC Memory wire

This is used to make central stamens for the flower. Cut to size, allowing extra length for insertion into the body of the fabric, and then secure by stitching on the back. Curl the end using flat nose pliers to create the top of the stamen. Add a tiny piece of fabric glue to stop it from fraying.

Fabric

For the main body of the embroidery

You will need a good quality linen, preferably of an even weave, and a backing fabric such as muslin or calico. It is important to have a good backing fabric to help support the wired elements of the embroidery.

I recommend you wash the fabrics before you start working with them, especially if you think you might ever need to wash the piece in the future.

Then baste the pieces together, making sure the grains of the fabric are running together.

For the stumpwork elements

Select lightweight cotton fabrics such as calico or lawn.

Stiletto

This is an essential piece of equipment for stumpwork. It is used to make holes in the main body of the fabric, to insert the wires to the back of the piece. It helps move the threads to the side of the fabric, avoiding an unsightly hole.

DMC six-strand floss

I used colours 552, 554, 470 and 472 for this piece. Feel free to use other colours that you prefer. Two strands of DMC were used throughout this project, except for the stems where three strands were used.

Fabric pens

I used Spectrum Noir colour CG2 for the leaves. This is sold in a set but any good quality fabric pen will do for the project in this book.

Glue

Any good fabric or craft glue. I highly recommend a general craft glue made by Hemline.

Other equipment

Use flat nosed pliers to adjust the wire, and a pair of wire cutters or old scissors to cut it.

You will also need the usual embroidery equipment: needles, scissors, tacking thread, pins and embroidery frame.

When you have your cloth, back it with a piece of muslin. You can tack these pieces together; all tacking will be removed after the work has been finished.

Designing for stumpwork embroidery

When I design a new piece, I start by looking at photographs and the actual flower itself. It is helpful to think about how flowers grow and how they are made up of simple shapes.

I often make a watercolour painting of the flower I'm planning to create; if you make a simple line drawing of the finished shape you're aiming for, then this will help you achieve a good result.

If you don't feel confident enough to draw your own design, use the template on page 28. Use a printer to scale it up and down to the size you'd like.

Next, trace the shapes in your drawing. While doing this, think about which areas you would like to be raised and which you will embroider flat onto the background cloth.

^ *Create simple shapes for embroidery by tracing onto tracing paper.*

Tips & Tricks
Don't be frightened – using a pen can sometimes be easier than a pencil. Experiment with whatever medium you like to draw with.

Working your design

> Create a line drawing to follow.
> I produced this simple line drawing
> from my designs and observations
> from the previous pages. I broke
> the design down into two areas.
> The black line shows the flat areas
> that need to be drawn onto the
> background cloth. The purple lines
> show the stumpwork pieces to
> be worked.

> This is the line drawing that is being
> used for the project in this book.
> If you want to experiment with
> different stitches and size, this is
> the time to experiment. Think about
> what you want to achieve and the
> end purpose of the piece.

> Now we are ready to start the design
> illustrated in this book. Transfer the
> design onto the base fabric, ideally
> a linen of an even weave. Edinburgh
> linen 36 count was used in the
> project shown. Use a soluble pen to
> draw directional lines on the leaves
> to help work the direction
> of stitching.

Tips & Tricks
Use a light box or
attach the pieces to
a window to transfer
your design.

How to make the stumpwork petals

We start with the petals. The techinique shown here can be used for both petals and leaves. To keep things simple we are showing how to make the stumpwork petal for the project shown in this book.

Work out the desired height of your petal, then cut a piece of wire five-times as long. So, if you want your finished size to be 2.5cm, then the length of the wire should be 12.5cm.

Cut six lengths: one for each petal.

∨ *Use wire cutters or a pair of old scissors to cut your wire.*

Shaping the wire

1. Using the petal template as a guide, take your flat nose pliers and fold the wire in half; this creates the top of the petal. The petal I've used here is 2.5cm in height.

2. Cross over the two ends of the wires at the bottom point of the template.

3. Uncross the wires and cut the outer wire just above the bend. Fold the inner wire upwards about 3mm and cut.

> ### Tips & Tricks
> Try to handle the wire as little as possible: the more you handle it the more it will distort.

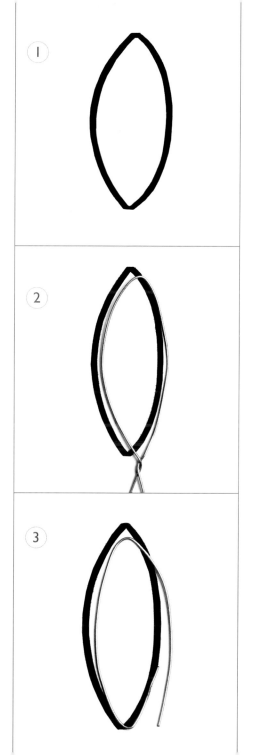

4. Couch the wire onto the calico. Draw directional lines with a 2H pencil or soluble pen as a guide to follow for your stitching.

5. Work long and short stitch, using two strands of DMC thread. After the thread is secured, take the needle from the centre line about a third down, up through the cloth. Then, insert the needle at the top point of the petal, inside the wire shape, and work a slightly shorter stitch in the same way next to the previous stitch. Repeat the process, moving from the centre to the right, fanning the stitches out so that you are following the growing pencil line of the petal, to about two-thirds down. Work the other side, starting at the top and working to the left.

6. Complete a second row in the same colour. This time, bring the needle through the previous row of stitching, trying to fit into the long and short stitches from the first row. Always make the stitches slightly longer as this helps blend the threads.

Tips & Tricks
When embroidering, make sure you take the needle right to the inner wire edge, so many of my students leave too large a gap and so the base cloth will be seen in the finished piece.

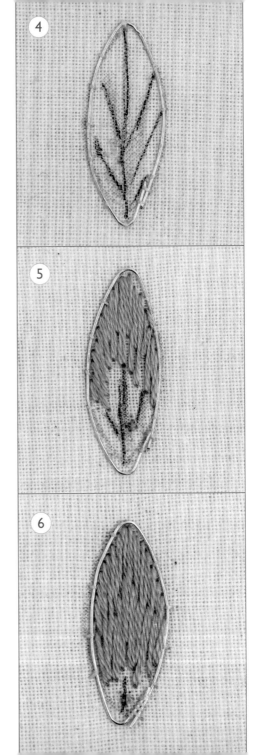

7. For the last row of stitching, change to the second colour. Work as the previous rows, from the centre to the right and then from the centre to the left. Always secure the end of the thread with a double stitch, or thread the needle through the previous work and cut off the excess.

8. Buttonhole the outer edge from the left side, incorporating the wire. It is really important to change the colour where the shading changes. This helps to create greater depth. You can thread the new colour though the loop made, then take the remaining thread to the other side of the petal to be picked up again to complete the buttonhole stitch.

9. If you want to add further detail to the petal, then this is the time to do it. You could use a metallic thread and add french knots or some straight lines, indicating petal lines.

10. Cut out the petals leaving 3mm around the edge. Using a good fabric glue and maybe a cocktail stick, push the excess fabric to the back of the petal.

11. You can manipulate the fabric so the buttonhole stitch stands out from the edge to create a clean finish. You should end with a petal that can be bent and moved to create a 3D effect onto your embroidery.

12. If you feel confident, an alternative way to finish the petal is to cut the excess fabric away up to the buttonhole stitch. Taking care not to cut the buttonhole stitching itself, as this can lead to a slightly fluffy finish around the edge of the piece.

If you need further help on how to stitch long and short, please refer to the stitch guide at the back of the book.

Tips & Tricks
Use Hemline's Fabric Craft and General adhesive. Squeeze some on a piece of paper first and transfer using a cocktail stick. This will ensure that there is not too much glue transferred to the petal shape, to help maintain its flexibility.

How to make the stumpwork leaf

For this technique, the embroidery thread is taken over the edge of the wire, rather than within. This means that there is no buttonhole stitching. There is also a tail of wire, which will help create the stem. This enables the leaf to stand proud from the background fabric.

Don't forget, this method can also be used for petals.

1. Couch the wire to the calico using a matching dressmaker's cotton, like you did for the petal. leaving the tail of the wire free. Draw the directional lines and the central vein of the leaf onto the fabric, using a 2H pencil or a soluble pen.

2. Use two strands of DMC thread and secure the thread. Work some running stitching on the left side of the leaf, as shown, as this helps to stop the embroidery collapsing into itself. Start a little way down from the central line, working towards the top. Take the needle from the central vein line over the outer edge of the wire. Insert the needle at an angle, almost inserting the needle under the wire edge. Follow the lines drawn in and work towards the bottom of the shape, making sure you cover the wire. If you see a gap, don't be frightened to go back and insert another stitch.

3. Repeat the process on the other side.

If you need further help on stitches, please refer to the stitch guide at the back of the book.

4. Finish the satin stitch over the wire edge, as shown on the other side.

5. Stitch some vein lines using split stitch. Wind the remaining thread around the two tails of wire, creating a stem for your piece. Tie off the end but do not cut off the excess thread, as this will be used to sew the wire to the backing cloth when the wire is inserted.

6. Now cut out the leaves leaving 3mm all the way around the leaf.

∧ *You can colour the calico with a fabric pen to help blend the backing fabric with the stitching.*

7. Turn back the excess calico, glueing it as you go. Use a cocktail stick if it helps.

8. Here is the back of my finished leaf, once the calico has been glued down.

9. Front of the leaf showing the veining and the final finish you are aiming to achieve. The tail of thread is left on to sew the wire to the backing cloth when the leaf is inserted into the main body of the embroidery.

Finishing your stumpwork

Stumpwork leaf inserted into the main body

Arrange and sew the petals down to the main body of the fabric. Use a matching thread and sew the bottom of the petals down only

Leaf worked in satin stitch and split stitch for veining

Whipped stem stitch to be used for stems

Finishing

Use two strands of the DMC thread for the satin, split and running stitches. Three strands are used for the stems. Embroider all the stems in whipped stem stitch. Use dark green for the stem and lighter green for the whipped element of the stitch.

Split stitch around the 'flat' leaves, add the running stitches as shown. Then satin stitch over the leaves covering the split stitch.

1. To attach the stumpwork leaf, make a hole in the fabric from the front of the cloth using the stiletto.

2. Insert the wire and then push the base fabric back to cover the hole. Fold the wire down the stem line on the back of the piece.

> **Tips & Tricks**
> You can embroider the flat leaves before or after you insert the stumpwork leaf, but work the stem lines so you have an area to sew the wire on the back of the piece.

3. Sew the wire that has been inserted into the back to the backing cloth. Cut off the excess wire when you feel the piece has been made firmly secured.

4. Here you can see the leaf firmly attached to the embroidered piece.

5. Now attach the petals. Carefully arrange them in a circle as shown. Sew the petals to the fabric with a few stitches at the bottom of each petal. Use one strand of embroidery floss in the matching colour.

Tips & Tricks
Shape the stumpwork pieces before you stitch them into place. It is far harder to do this once they are attached to the background fabric.

6. Work french knots or beads in the centre of the flower. If you want to create a truly 3D effect, use DMC memory wire to make stamens. Remember to glue the end to prevent it from unravelling.

7. The memory wire stamens are inserted into the fabric in a similar fashion to the stumpwork leaf. Use your stiletto to create the hole for the ends of the wire to be inserted into the background cloth. Secure the ends of the memory wire with some stitches to the back of the cloth.

Inspirational ideas

I encourage you to use these techniques and take them a step further in your own creations.

Here are some projects I've made, using these techniques to create unique presents. This brooch (see right) could be adapted to make a special flower or corsage for a groom to wear on their wedding day.

< I used the the template for the petals to decorate the top of a box, made as a present for a friend.

Extras for your projects

Tendrils (see picture, right) can be made by wrapping thread around wire. You can start off with a few wires and then twist them together to create greater interest.

This flower was made out of two pieces of Liberty fabric fused together, stitched and then cut out close to the edge of the buttonhole stitching. I used hat maker's stamens to create interest in the middle of the flower.

I made the petals with long wire stems so I could twist them together. Then I covered the wires with stranded cotton, applying a little glue at the end to secure the thread.

Berries

You can make berries by sewing around a bead: just make sure the bead has a large hole to accomadate the thread. Tie the thread around the bead leaving a tail, as this gives you something to hold onto while you stitch the bead.

You can finish the beads in various ways: a bead, a french knot or a few straight stiches as shown. You can insert a wire wrapped in thread into the bottom of the bead if you need a stem. A little glue might need to be added to help secure it in place.

Stitch Techniques

Long & Short Stitch

The first row of stitching must be worked tightly together, so you see no background cloth. Start by securing your thread, then bring the needle up through the cloth on the central line about a third down from the top of the shape. Keep inside the wired outline. Draw directional lines using a 2H pencil or soluble pen if it helps. Always work towards the growing point, except the first row where you work from the inside to the outline.

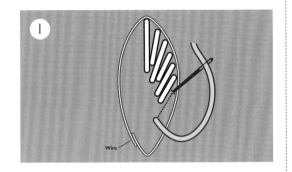

When the first row is completed, come up through the previous stitches, this helps the stitches to blend together for the second row. Continue around the shape as you did for the first row. Vary the length of your stitches and make each stitch longer than you want to make it. Always go up into the previous stitch higher than you think — be generous. This helps to achieve good coverage and hide the base cloth.

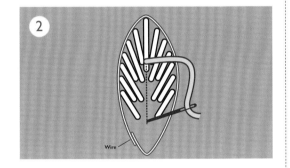

Now complete the third row again, coming up through the previous row of stitches as before. You may need to add more rows of stitching if your piece is larger than this guide.

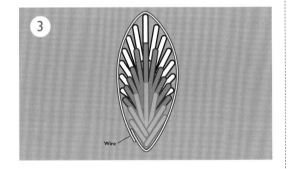

Buttonhole Stitch

Buttonhole stitch is used to cover the wire for the petals. Stitch as close as you can. Start from the bottom left and work around the shape. The looped edge makes a good clean edge for the petal. The thread appears on the outer edge and then the needle is taken over the wire and inserted into the fabric covering the wire; leave the thread loose so you can then bring the needle up through the fabric to catch the thread, creating a loop. Pull tight and repeat, covering the wire.

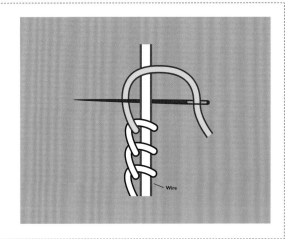

French Knots

These can be used in a contrasting thread to add interest to the petals. Bring the thread up through the fabric where you require the knot to be. Then twist the thread around the needle two or three times, depending on how large you want the knot, as shown in step 1.

Pull the thread so it is fairly tight around the needle and hold the remaining thread tightly in the left hand, turn the point of the needle completely around and inserted it back into the ground just by where the thread first emerged, as shown in step 2.

Pull the needle down into the cloth and if it helps keep your left index finger on top of the needle as you pull the needle though. The key to success is to try and keep even twists around the needle and when you turn the needle to insert back into the fabric keep a good tension.

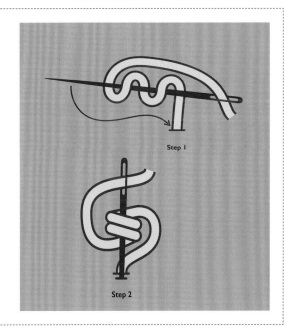

Satin Stitch

Work a straight stitch. Follow the directional lines. Make the slant of the stitch greater than you think. Bring the needle up at the central line, a third of the way down. Take the needle over the wire or split stitched outline. Try and angle the needle going under the outer edge of the wire or split stitch. Work towards the top, and then work the bottom section from the middle downwards. Add a few small stitches on the bottom to prevent the upper stitches collapsing.

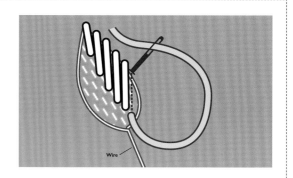

Split Stitch

Split stitch can be used to outline the flat leaf shapes and for the veins of the leaves. The needle emerges from the material and then taken back into the fabric, creating a stitch. The needle is then inserted back up through the stitch, splitting the stitch.

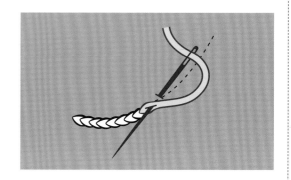

Slanted Stem Stitch

Bring the needle up through the fabric and hold the thread to the left, then bring the needle back through the cloth halfway along where the next stitch will be worked. Pull the thread through the fabric and repeat.

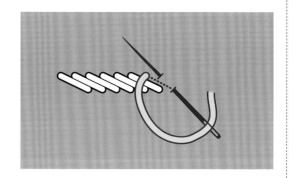

Whipped Stem Stitch

Whipped stem stitch is used for the stems. You first work a row of slanted stem and then you 'whip' a thread around the stem stitch to create a raised effect. The needle should not enter the material but instead insert it in and out of the stem stitch as shown in the illustration.

The project in this book uses the dark green for the stem and the lighter green for the whipping.

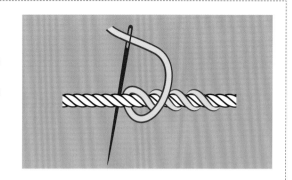

Running Stitch

Running stitch is worked before the satin stitch to create padding. This helps the satin stitch from collapsing into itself.

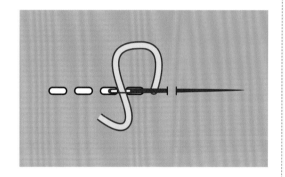

Straight Stitch

Use a contrasting thread to add further interest to the petals using a straight stitch as illustrated.

A silver thread was used for the project in this book.

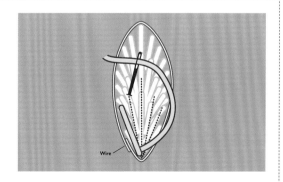

Templates

Template for the flat work

You can increase or decrease the size of these templates with the aid of a photocopier, if you wish.

For this project, the petals I worked on were 2.5cm tall and the leaves were 2cm.

> ### Tips & Tricks
> *It's good to practise on a larger shape first to help build your confidence.*

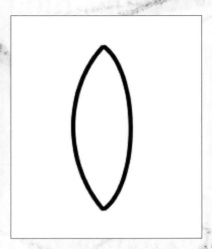

Petal template for the wire shape

Leaf template for the wire shape

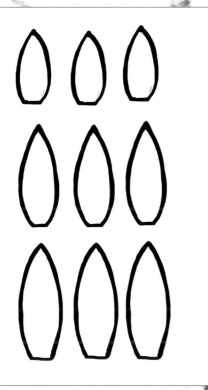

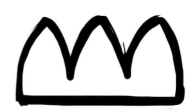

Felt template

The top template is made out of felt. Roll it up after it's been cut out, secure with glue and then wrap the wired leaves around it.

Wired leaf templates for the succulent plant

I recommend you photocopy this page and play around with the size you would like your plant to be.

For this project, remember to leave tails on the wires so you can twist the leaves together.

I used a plain green cotton cloth that the wires were couched down onto.